BOLD KIDS

AF323380

Rainforest Animals

EDUCATIONAL FACTS
CHILDREN'S ANIMAL BOOK

This book is not intended to be a complete list of rainforest animals. However, you will find several interesting ones to learn about, including the Tapir, Maues marmoset, and the army ant.

Keep reading for more information about these amazing animals! And remember, you are not alone!

TAPIR

Tapirs are one of the top trophic levels of the rainforest, sharing their habitat with other species. These nocturnal animals are very useful to the forest ecosystem by dispersing seeds and fruit from trees.

They also have a unique protuberance on their upper lip that resembles a small trunk, which they use to catch leaves and other foods. This animal is also able to breathe underwater, using a prensile organ.

MAUES MARMOSET

The Maues marmoset is endemic to the Amazon region of Brazil. Its home is the west bank of the Rio Maues-Acu, and it can be found only in the state of Amazonas.

It has a black circumbuccal zone on its face, heavy silver-brown fur lining its ears, and a faint orange tint to its tail. It eats fruits, gums, and small animals.

CHEETAH

Cheetahs are large cats that are fast and agile. They are larger than leopards but not as heavy. Their body length is around 1.5m (5ft), and their tails add another 85cm (33in).

Their shoulder height is about 80 to 90 inches. They weigh between 50 and 64kg. Despite their large size, they are very quiet animals. They purr like domestic cats, and do not roar.

KOMODO DRAGON

The Komodo dragon is a species of rainforest animal that lives in Indonesia.

It is the dominant animal in the island and eats a variety of prey including deer, water buffalo, pigs, insects, geckos, and smaller lizards.

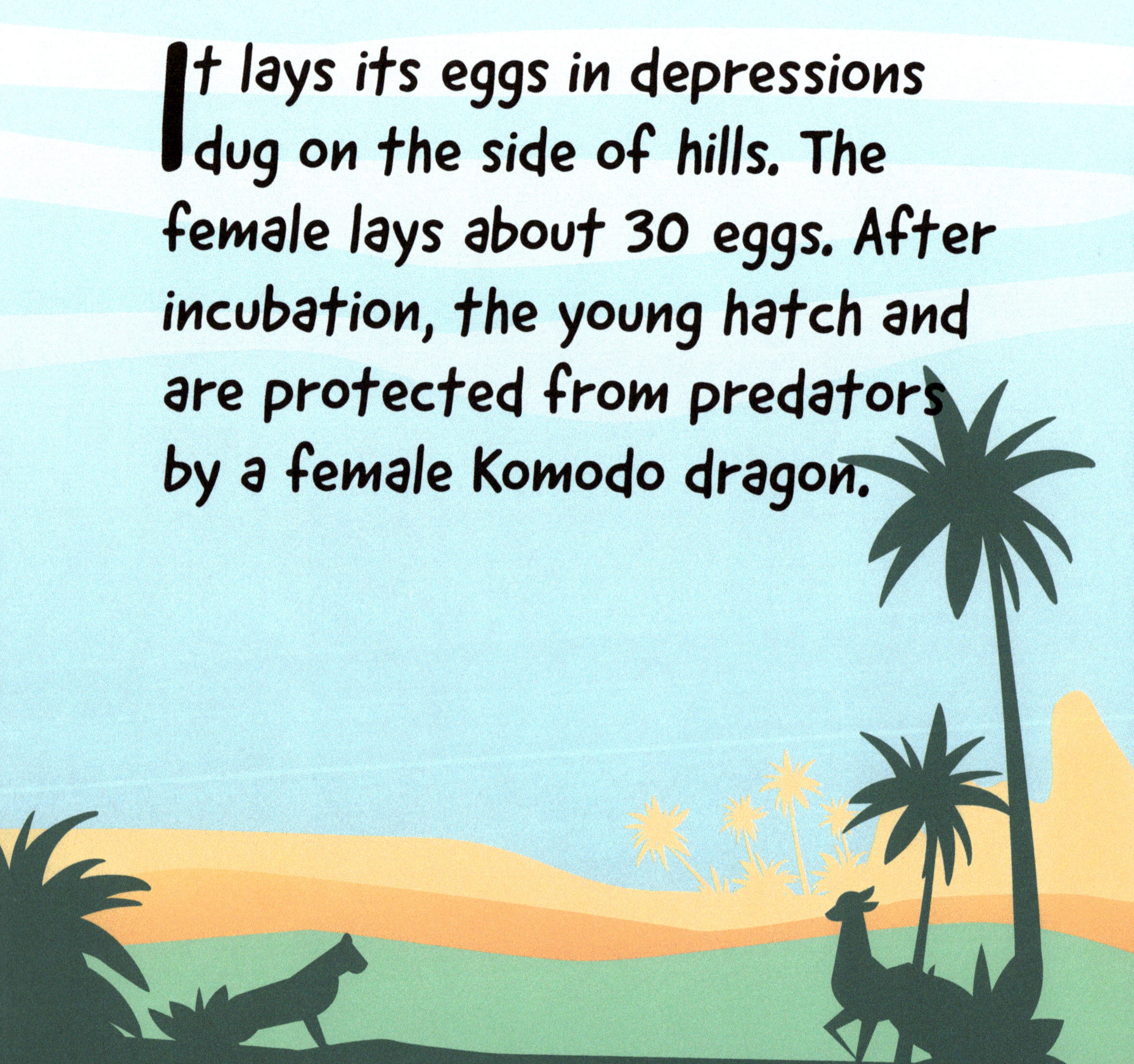

It lays its eggs in depressions dug on the side of hills. The female lays about 30 eggs. After incubation, the young hatch and are protected from predators by a female Komodo dragon.

The Komodo dragon breeds from September to March and the young survive for approximately five to seven years. A female will stop reproducing around thirty years of age.

CHAMELEON

If you're an animal lover, you might be intrigued by the Chameleon. This reptile has some very unique features, and one of the most amazing features is its amazing eyes.

Its eyes are the most distinct of all reptiles, and have scaly lids and a tiny round pupil. Unlike other reptiles, the Chameleon is able to look at two things at once, allowing it to keep a 360-degree field of vision.

JEWEL BEETLE

In the rainforests of Australia, jewel beetles are a common sight. Their stunning color and design make them a striking sight.

The insects live in all habitats, from lowland rainforests to high alpine regions. Some of them are edible, while others are used for art, jewelry, textiles, and biological control.

POISON DART FROG

Poison dart frogs are members of the family Dendrobatidae. They are brightly colored to warn predators of their toxicity.

These frogs are relatively small and have flattened tips. They prefer to live in leaf litter and rest on tree branches.

CPSIA information can be obtained
at www.ICGtesting.com
Printed in the USA
LVHW071737270123
738092LV00008B/289